"This lovely, easy-to [...]
cipleship in the glow[...]
to think that as we grow as Christians, we move on to 'higher things' (whatever that means!), when in fact we simply need to learn the beauty and depth of Jesus and all that he's done for us. That's what Ortlund helps us do here. This book will bless you!"

Paul E. Miller, author, *A Praying Life* and *J-Curve: Dying and Rising with Jesus in Everyday Life*

"That angst in your soul for more is a part of the growing process— a gift of hunger and thirst that Jesus, the inexhaustible well, will fill. In *How Does God Change Us?*, Dane Ortlund reminds us that the angst is satisfied not by behavioral modification or some quick fix but by the beauty of friendship with Jesus and the peace more deeply accepted in our souls. If you are hungry and thirsty for more life, more joy, more peace, and more Jesus, this is a book for you."

Matt Chandler, Lead Pastor, The Village Church, Dallas, Texas; President, Acts 29 Church Planting Network; author, *The Mingling of Souls* and *The Explicit Gospel*

"Jesus said that our greatest 'work' is to believe. As much as any living author, Dane Ortlund has helped me to believe again by reacquainting me with the stunning tenderness and beauty of Jesus. As I read his words, I can sense my heart growing in trust, devotion, and godly affections, grounded in the Savior's love for me. In this incredibly helpful, pastoral book, Dane works out the implications of that vision of Jesus for personal growth, showing us how the key to going further with Jesus is going deeper in his finished work."

J. D. Greear, Lead Pastor, The Summit Church, Raleigh-Durham, North Carolina

"How does God change us as his beloved daughters and sons? Think less of climbing a mountain and more of swimming in a deep ocean of the always-more-ness of Jesus. If you've ever wondered what the Bible really means by 'fixing our gaze on Jesus, the author and perfecter of our faith,' this should be the next book you spend time with. Dane helps us understand that the gospel is more of a person to adore and know than theological propositions and categories to master."

Scotty Smith, Pastor Emeritus, Christ Community Church, Franklin, Tennessee; Teacher in Residence, West End Community Church, Nashville, Tennessee

HOW DOES GOD CHANGE US?

Union

A book series edited by Michael Reeves

Rejoice and Tremble: The Surprising Good News of the Fear of the Lord, Michael Reeves (2021)

What Does It Mean to Fear the Lord?, Michael Reeves (2021, concise version of *Rejoice and Tremble*)

Deeper: Real Change for Real Sinners, Dane C. Ortlund (2021)

How Does God Change Us?, Dane C. Ortlund (2021, concise version of *Deeper*)

HOW DOES GOD CHANGE US?

DANE C. ORTLUND

WHEATON, ILLINOIS

How Does God Change Us?
Copyright © 2021 by Dane C. Ortlund
Published by Crossway
    1300 Crescent Street
    Wheaton, Illinois 60187

Cover design: Jordan Singer

Cover image: Museum Purchase, Gallery Fund / Bridgeman Images

First printing 2021

Printed in the United States of America

Scripture quotations are from the ESV® Bible (The Holy Bible, English Standard Version®), copyright © 2001 by Crossway, a publishing ministry of Good News Publishers. Used by permission. All rights reserved.

Trade paperback ISBN: 978-1-4335-7403-0
ePub ISBN: 978-1-4335-7405-4
PDF ISBN: 978-1-4335-7404-7
Mobipocket ISBN: 978-1-4335-7406-1

Library of Congress Cataloging-in-Publication Data

Names: Ortlund, Dane Calvin, author.
Title: How does God change us? / Dane C. Ortlund.
Description: Wheaton, Illinois : Crossway, [2021] | Series: Union | Includes bibliographical
 references and index.
Identifiers: LCCN 2021002413 (print) | LCCN 2021002414 (ebook) | ISBN
 9781433574030 (trade paperback) | ISBN 9781433574047 (epdf) | ISBN
 9781433574061 (mobi) | ISBN 9781433574054 (epub)
Subjects: LCSH: Change (Psychology)—Religious aspects—Christianity. | Habit breaking—
 Religious aspects—Christianity. | Sin—Christianity.
Classification: LCC BV4599.5.C44 O78 2021 (print) | LCC BV4599.5.C44 (ebook) | DDC
 233—dc23
LC record available at https://lccn.loc.gov/2021002413
LC ebook record available at https://lccn.loc.gov/2021002414

Crossway is a publishing ministry of Good News Publishers.

VP   30 29 28 27 26 25 24 23 22 21
15 14 13 12 11 10 9 8 7 6 5 4 3 2 1

Affectionately dedicated to
the faculty of Covenant Theological Seminary, 2002–2006,
who taught me about real change from the Bible,
then showed me with their lives

"Aslan," said Lucy, "you're bigger."

"That is because you are older, little one," answered he.

"Not because you are?"

"I am not. But every year you grow, you will find me bigger."

C. S. LEWIS, *Prince Caspian*

Contents

Series Preface

OUR INNER CONVICTIONS AND VALUES shape our lives and our ministries. And at Union—the cooperative ministries of Union School of Theology, Union Publishing, Union Research, and Union Mission (visit www.theolo.gy)—we long to grow and support men and women who will delight in God, grow in Christ, serve the church, and bless the world. This Union series of books is an attempt to express and share those values.

They are values that flow from the beauty and grace of God. The living God is so glorious and kind, he cannot be known without being adored. Those who truly know him will love him, and without that heartfelt delight in God, we are nothing but hollow hypocrites. That adoration of God necessarily works itself out in a desire to grow in Christlikeness. It also fuels a love for Christ's precious bride, the church, and a desire humbly to serve—rather than use—her. And, lastly, loving God brings us to share his concerns, especially to see his life-giving glory fill the earth.

Each exploration of a subject in the Union series will appear in two versions: a full volume and a concise one. The concise treatments, such as this one, are like shorter guided tours: they stick to the main streets and move on fast. You may find, at the end of this little book, that you have questions or want to explore some more: in that case, the fuller volume will take you further up and further in.

My hope and prayer is that these books will bless you and your church as you develop a deeper delight in God that overflows in joyful integrity, humility, Christlikeness, love for the church, and a passion to make disciples of all nations.

Michael Reeves
SERIES EDITOR

Introduction

THE BIBLE SAYS, "GROW in the grace and knowledge of our Lord and Savior Jesus Christ" (2 Pet. 3:18). But how do we do that? How does God actually change us?

The basic point of this little book is that change is a matter of going deeper. Some believers think change happens through outward improvement—behaving more and more in accord with some moral norm (the biblical law, or the commands of Jesus, or conscience, or whatever). Others think change happens mainly through intellectual addition—understanding doctrine with greater breadth and precision. Others think it comes centrally through felt experience—sensory increase as we worship God.

All three of these elements are included in healthy Christian development (and if any is missing, we are out of proportion and will not grow), but real growth transcends them all. Growing in Christ is not centrally improving or adding or experiencing but *deepening*. Implicit in the notion of deepening is that you already have what you need. Christian growth is bringing what you do and say and even feel into line with what, in fact, you already are.

Let me be clear: We're not after behavior modification in this book. I'm not going to talk to you about setting your alarm earlier or cutting carbs. We're not even going to reflect on tithing or church attendance or journaling or small groups or taking the sacraments or reading the Puritans. All of that can be done out of rottenness of heart. We're talking about *real* change. And we're talking about real change for *real sinners*.

A few things right up front.

First, I'm not going to hurry you. No one else should either. We are complicated sinners. Sometimes we take two steps forward and three steps back. We need time. Be patient with yourself. A sense of urgency, yes; but not a sense of hurry. Overnight transformations are the exception, not the norm. Slow change is still real change.

Second, as you begin this book, open your heart to the possibility of real change in your life. One of the devil's great victories is to flood our hearts with a sense of futility. Perhaps his greatest victory in your life is not a sin you are habitually committing but simply a sense of helplessness as to real growth.

Third, this book is written by a fellow patient, not a doctor. It is written to me as much as by me. Out of failure as much as out of success.

1

Jesus

THIS IS A BOOK about growing in Christ. The first thing to get clear, then, is what Jesus Christ himself is like. Our growth is not independent personal improvement. It is growth *in Christ*. Who then is he?

The temptation for many of us at this point is to assume we pretty much know what Jesus is like. We've been saved by him. We've spent time in the Bible over the years. We've read some books about him. We've told a few others about him.

And yet, if we are honest, we still find our lives riddled with failure and worry and dysfunction and emptiness.

One common reason we fail to leave sin behind is that we have a domesticated view of Jesus. Not an unorthodox view; we are fully orthodox in our Christology. We understand that he came from heaven as the Son of God to live the life we cannot live and die the death we deserve to die. We affirm his glorious resurrection. We confess with the ancient creeds that he is truly God and truly man. We don't have a heterodox view. We have a domesticated view that, for all its doctrinal precision, has down-sized the glory of Christ in our hearts.. We have forgotten that the Bible speaks of "the *unsearchable* riches of Christ" (Eph. 3:8).

So we need to begin by getting clear on who this person is in whom we grow. And we start just there—he is a person. Not just a historical figure, but an actual person, alive and well today. He is to be related to. Trusted, spoken to, listened to. Jesus is not a concept. Not an ideal. Not a force. Growing in Christ is a relational, not a formulaic, experience.

In this chapter I want to mention just one truth about Jesus, perhaps the most neglected and also the most vital truth about him if you are to get real traction in growing spiritually: Jesus is tender with us.

Tender

Jesus Christ is infinitely gentle. He is the most open and accessible, the most peaceful and accommodating person in the universe. He is the most tender, least abrasive person you will ever come across. Infinite strength, infinite meekness. Dazzlingly resplendent; endlessly calm.

If you had only a few words to define who Jesus is, what would you say? In the one place where he himself tells us about his own heart, he says, "I am gentle and lowly in heart" (Matt. 11:29). And remember that the "heart" in biblical terms is not merely our emotions but the innermost animating center of all that we do. Our deepest loves and desires and ambitions pour out of our hearts. And when Jesus opens himself up and tells us of the fountain, the engine, the throbbing core of all that he does, he says that deeper than anything else, he is gentle and lowly. Peer down into the deepest recesses of Jesus Christ and there we find: gentleness and lowliness.

We who know our hearts resist this. We see the ugliness within. We can hardly face ourselves, we feel so inadequate. And Jesus is perfectly holy, the divine Son of God. It is normal and natural, even in our churches, to sense instinctively that he is holding his people at arm's length. This is why we need a Bible. The testimony of the entire Bible, culminating in Matthew 11:29, is that God defies what we instinctively feel by embracing his people in their mess. He finds penitence, distress, need, and lack irresistible.

You don't have to go through security to get to Jesus. You don't have to get in line or take a ticket. No waving for his attention. No raising your voice to make sure he hears you.

In your smallness, he notices you. In your sinfulness, he draws near to you. In your anguish, he is in solidarity with you.

What we must see is not only that Jesus is gentle toward you but that he is positively drawn toward you when you are most sure he doesn't want to be. It's not only that he is not repelled by your fallenness—he finds your need and emptiness and sorrow irresistible. He is not slow to meet you in your need. It's the difference between a teenager's alarm going off on a Monday morning, forcing him to drag himself out of bed, and that same teen springing out of bed on Christmas morning. Just look at the Savior in Matthew, Mark, Luke, and John. With whom does he hang out? What draws forth his tears? What gets him out of bed in the morning? With whom does he eat lunch? The sidelined, the hollowed out, those long out of hope, those who have sent their lives into meltdown.

The Real Jesus

The first thing I want to make clear here, early in this book, is that the real Jesus is gentle and lowly in heart. I say the *real* Jesus because we all unwittingly dilute him. We cut him down to what our minds can naturally imagine. But the Bible corrects us, tells us to stop doing that. We can only create a Jesus in our own image—a Jesus of moderate gentleness and mercy—without a Bible. Scripture tears down that diluted Jesus and lets loose the real Christ. And what we find is that his deepest heart is gentle and lowly.

This is a book about how we change. Let me be plain. *You will not change until you get straight who Jesus is, particularly with regard to his surprising tenderness.* And then spend your whole life long going deeper into the gentleness of Jesus. The only alternative to the real Jesus is to get back on the treadmill—the treadmill of doing your best to follow and honor Jesus but believing his mercy and grace to be a stockpile gradually depleted by your failures, and hoping to make it to death before the mountain of mercy runs out. Here is the teaching of the Bible: If you are in Christ, your sins cause that stockpile to grow all the more. Where sins abound, his grace superabounds. It is in your pockets of deepest shame and regret that his heart dwells *and won't leave.*

As you read this book and as you continue to work your way through life, shed once and for all the reduced Jesus and lift your eyes to the real Jesus, the Jesus whose tenderness ever outstrips and embraces your weaknesses, the Christ whose riches are unsearchable. This Christ is one under whose care and instruction you will finally be able to blossom and grow.

2

Despair

THERE IS A STRANGE though consistent message throughout the Bible. We are told time and again that the way forward will feel like we're going backward.

The Psalms tell us that those whose hearts are breaking and who feel crushed by life are the people God is closest to (Ps. 34:18). Proverbs tells us it is to the low and the destitute that God shows favor (Prov. 3:34). In Isaiah we are surprised to learn that God dwells in two places: way up high, in the glory of heaven, and way down low, with those void of self-confidence and empty of themselves (Isa. 57:15; 66:1–2). Jesus tells us that "unless a grain of wheat falls into the earth and dies, it remains alone; but if it dies, it bears much fruit" (John 12:24).

Why does the Bible do this? Does God want us always feeling bad about ourselves?

Not at all. It is because of God's very desire that we be joyously happy, filled to overflowing with the uproarious cheer of heaven itself, that he says these things. For he is sending us down into honesty and sanity. He wants us to see our sickness so we can run to the doctor. He wants us to get healed.

Fallen human beings enter into joy only through the door of despair. Fullness can be had only through emptiness. That happens decisively at conversion, as we confess our hopelessly sinful predicament for the first time and collapse into the arms of Jesus, and then remains an ongoing rhythm throughout the Christian life. If you are not growing in Christ, one reason may be that you have drifted out of the salutary and healthy discipline of self-despair.

The Great Prerequisite

If you feel stuck, defeated by old sin patterns, leverage that despair into the healthy sense of self-futility that is the door through which you must pass if you are to get real spiritual traction. Let your emptiness humble you. Let it take you *down*.

We will come to the positive counterparts to this death in chapters ahead. But we cannot circumvent this stage. It is the great prerequisite to everything else. The pattern of the Christian life is not a straight line up to resurrection existence but a curve down into death and thereby up into resurrection existence. And one thing that means is that we go through life with an ever-deepening sense of how reprehensible, in ourselves, we really are. It was toward the *end* of his life that Paul identified himself as the most award-winning sinner he knew (1 Tim. 1:15). The godliest octogenarians I know are those who feel themselves to be more sinful now than at any time before. They have known the pattern of healthy self-despair. Who of us cannot relate to what the pastor and hymn-writer John Newton wrote in a 1776 letter (at age fifty-one): "The life of faith seems so simple and easy in theory, that I can point it out to others in few words; but in practice it is very difficult, and my advances are so slow, that I hardly dare say I get forward at all."[1]

Have you been brought to despair of what you can achieve in your sanctification? If not, have the courage to look yourself squarely in the mirror. Repent. See your profound poverty. Ask the Lord to forgive your arrogance. As you descend down into death, into knowledge of the futility of what inner change you can achieve by your own efforts, it is there, right there, in that dismay and emptiness, *that God lives*. It is there in that desert that he loves to cause the waters to flow and the trees to bloom. Your despair is all he needs to work with. "Only acknowledge your guilt" (Jer. 3:13). What will ruin your growth is if you look the other way, if you deflect the searching gaze of Purity himself, if you cover over your sinfulness and emptiness with smiles and jokes and then go check your mutual funds again, holding at bay what you know in your deepest heart: you are wicked.

If you plunge down only a little into self-despair, you will rise only a little into joyous growth in Christ. Don't just admit your condition is desperately ruinous. Let yourself feel it. Ponder, unhurriedly, how vile, left to yourself, you are.

Collapse

But as we despair of our own capacities to generate growth—what then?

There is nothing noble about staying in that pit of despair. Healthy despair is an intersection, not a highway; a gateway, not a pathway. We must go there. But we dare not stay there.

The Bible teaches, rather, that each experience of despair is to melt us afresh into deeper fellowship with Jesus. Like jumping on a trampoline, we are to go down into freshly felt emptiness but then let that spring us high into fresh heights with Jesus. The Bible calls this two-step movement repentance and faith.

Repentance is turning from Self. Faith is turning to Jesus. You can't have one without the other. Repentance that does not turn to Jesus is not real repentance; faith that has not first turned from Self is not real faith. If we are traveling the wrong direction, things get fixed as we turn away from the wrong direction and simultaneously begin going the right direction. Both happen together.

Some Christians seem to think that the Christian life is ignited with a decisive act of repentance and then fed by faith thereafter. But as Luther taught, all of life is repentance. The first thesis of his Ninety-Five Theses reads, "When our Lord and Master Jesus Christ said, 'Repent' (Matt. 4:17), he willed the entire life of believers to be one of repentance." The Christian life is one of *repenting our way forward*.

Equally, we live our whole lives by faith. Paul said not "I was converted by faith" but "I live by faith" (Gal. 2:20). We do not merely begin the Christian life by faith; we progress by faith. It is our new normal. We process life, we navigate this mortal existence, by a moment-by-moment turning to God in trust and hope at each juncture, each decision, each passing hour. We "walk by faith, not by sight" (2 Cor. 5:7). That is, we move through life with our eyes looking ever up.

Repentance and faith. In a word: collapse.

Both repentance and faith, however, must never be viewed in isolation from Jesus himself. They are connectors to Christ. They are not "our contribution." They simply are the roads by which we get to real healing: Christ himself.

As you despair of yourself—agonizing over the desolation wrought by your failures, your weaknesses, your inadequacies—let that despair take you way down deep into honesty with yourself. For there you will find a friend, the living Lord Jesus himself, who will startle and surprise you with his gentle goodness as you leave Self behind, in repentance, and bank on him afresh, in faith.

3

Union

WE HAVE SHARPENED OUR VISION of who Jesus is. And we have established the ongoing salutary reality of self-despair and collapsing in penitent faith time and again into the arms of that Jesus. But does this Jesus remain at a distance? How do we actually access him?

The New Testament gives a resounding answer. Those who collapse into him in repentance and faith are united to him—joined to him—*one* with him. This is the controlling center, according to the New Testament, of what it means to be a Christian. And most fundamentally it is our union with Christ that, according to Scripture, fosters growth (e.g., Rom. 6:1–5).

Macro and Micro

But what does it mean to be "in" Christ?

The New Testament uses the language of union with Christ in basically two ways. We could call them the macro and the micro realities to union with Christ, or the cosmic and the intimate, or the federal and the personal.

The macro dimension to union with Christ is that he is your leader, and as he goes, so you go. His fate is yours. Why? Because you are *in* him. That may sound a little odd, especially for those of us who live in the West today. But for most human cultures throughout most of human history, including Bible times, this way of thinking about a leader and his people was normal and natural. The formal name for it is "corporate solidarity." If you've ever heard Christ referred to as believers' "federal" head, that's getting at the same notion. The idea is that the one represents the many, and the many are represented by the one.

We see it, for example, in 2 Corinthians 5:14, speaking of the work of Christ and how it connects to us: "One has died for all, therefore all have died." Because Christ died, and those united to him share in his fate, we too have "died" (see also Rom. 6:6, 8).

To be in Christ, then, in this macro or cosmic or federal way, is for our destiny to be bound up with his rather than with Adam's. First Corinthians 15:22 is the whole Bible in a short sentence: "As in Adam all die, so also in Christ shall all be made alive." The alternative to being in Christ is to be in Adam. One or the other. No third option. The most famous athletes, the cultural icons, those whose fans treat them like gods—what is most deeply true of them is that they are either in Adam or in Christ.

But there is a closer, more intimate reality to union with Christ—the micro dimension—and sometimes the biblical authors speak of our union in this way. It is difficult to know exactly how to express it. The Bible uses imagery to communicate it, perhaps because this reality is better likened than defined. We are given images such as a vine and its branches, or a head and the other body parts, or even a groom and his bride. In all cases there is an organic, intimate uniting, a sharing of properties, a oneness. The vine gives life to the branches; the head directs and cares for its body parts; the husband "nourishes and cherishes" his wife as he does his own body (Eph. 5:29; see also 1 Cor. 6:13–18).

Your salvation in the gospel is far deeper, far more wondrous, than walking an aisle or praying a prayer or raising a hand or going forward at an evangelistic rally. Your salvation is to be united to the living Christ himself. In that most intimate of unions, we are given back our true selves. You become the you that you were meant to be. You recover your original destiny. You realize that your existence out of Christ was a shadow of what you were made to be. In other words, it is only in union with Christ that you can grow into who God made you to be.

Safe and Secure

But how does our union with Christ actually foster growth and change?

How could it *not?* Note the sheer intimacy and safety of being a Christian. Our Christian growth takes place in the sphere of a wonderful inevitability, even invincibility. I am united to Christ. I can never be disunited from him. The logic of the New Testament letters is that in order for me to get disunited from Christ, Christ himself would have to be de-resurrected. He'd have to get kicked out of heaven for me to get kicked out of him. We're that safe.

Think of yourself as an onion. The outer peel consists of peripheral things about you, the parts of you that don't matter much: your clothes, the car you drive, things like that. If you peel away that layer, what's next? A collection of things slightly more essential to who you are: the family you were raised in, your personality profile, your blood type, your volunteer work. Peel that away. The next deeper layer is your relationships: your dearest friends, your roommates if you're a student, your spouse if you're married. Peel that away. The next deeper layer is what you believe about the world, the truths you cherish deep in your heart: who you believe God is, what your final future is, where you think world history is heading. The next deeper layer after that comprises your sins and secrets, past and present, things about you no one else knows.

Keep peeling away layer after layer, everything that makes you *you*. What do you find at the core? You are united to Christ. That is the most irreducible reality about you. Peel everything else away, and the solid, immovable truth about you is your union with a resurrected Christ.

Taking It Deep

Let your mind and heart go way down deep into the reality of your union with the living Lord Jesus Christ. If you are in him, you have everything you need to grow. By the Holy Spirit, you are in him and he is in you. He is both your federal head and your intimate companion. *You cannot lose.* You are inexhaustibly rich. For you are one with Christ, and he is himself inexhaustibly rich, the heir of the universe.

Submerge yourself in this truth. Let it wash over you. The divine Son, through whom all things were made (Col. 1:16), who "upholds the universe by the word of his power" (Heb. 1:3), is the one with whom you have been united. Through no activity of your own, but by the sheer and mighty grace of God, you have been enveloped in the triumphant and tender ruler of the cosmos.

Therefore: *nothing can touch you that does not touch him.* To get to you, every pain, every assault, every disappointment has to go through him. You are shielded by invincible love. He himself feels your anguish even more deeply than you do, because you're one with him; and he mediates everything hard in your life through his love for you, because you're one with him. Picture yourself standing in a circle with an invisible but impenetrable wall surrounding you, a sphere of impregnability. But it's not a circle you're in. It's a person—*the* person. The one before whom John fell down as he grappled for words to describe what he was looking at as one whose "eyes were like a flame of fire . . . and his voice was like the roar of many waters" (Rev. 1:14–15) has been made one with you. The might of heaven, the power that flung galaxies into existence, has swept you into himself.

And you're there to stay. Amid the storms of your little existence—the sins and sufferings, the failure and faltering, the waywardness and wandering—he is going to walk you right into heaven. He is not just with you. He is in you, and you in him. His destiny now falls on you. His union with you at both the macro and micro levels guarantees your eventual glory and rest and calm. You may as well question gravity as question the certainty of what your union with him means for your final future.

So consider the darkness that remains in your life. Our sins loom large. They seem so insurmountable. But Christ and your union with him loom larger still. As far as sin in your life reaches, Christ and your union with him reach further. As deep as your failure goes, Christ and your union with him go deeper still. Rest in the knowledge that your sins and failures can never kick you out of Christ. Let an ever-deepening awareness of your union with him strengthen your resistance to sin. See it in the Bible. Ponder his tireless care for you. You have been strengthened with the power to fight and overcome sin because the power that raised Jesus from the dead now resides in you, living and active—for Jesus Christ himself resides in you. You can never be justifiably accused ever again. "There is therefore now no condemnation for those who are *in* Christ Jesus" (Rom. 8:1).

Draw strength from your oneness with Jesus. You are no longer alone. No longer isolated. When you sin, don't give up. Let him pick you up and put you on your feet again with fresh dignity. He lifts your chin, looks you in the eye, and defines your existence: "you in me, and I in you" (John 14:20).

4

Embrace

THE FIRST THREE CHAPTERS have briefly laid a foundation—
Jesus Christ's gentleness (chap. 1), our emptiness (chap. 2), and our
union with him (chap. 3). Now we begin to get into the actual dy-
namics by which believers change. We begin with the love of God.

What is the love of God? To ask that question is the same as
to ask, what is God? The Bible says not simply that "God loves"
but also that "God is love" (1 John 4:8, 16). Love, for the God of
the Bible, is not one activity among others. Love defines who he
is most deeply. Ultimate reality is not cold, blank, endless space.
Ultimate reality is an eternal fountain of endless, unquenchable
love. A love so great and so free that it could not be contained
within the uproarious joy of Father, Son, and Spirit but spilled out
to create and embrace finite and fallen humans into it. Divine love

is inherently spreading, engulfing, embracing, overflowing. If you are a Christian, *God made you so that he could love you.*

What I want to say in this chapter is that the love of God is not something to see once and believe and then move beyond to other truths or strategies for growing in Christ. The love of God is what we feed on our whole lives long, wading ever more deeply into this endless ocean. And that feeding, that wading, is itself what fosters growth. *We grow in Christ no further than we enjoy his embrace of us.* His tender, mighty, irreversible embrace into his own divine heart.

The Unknowable Love of Christ

Paul didn't pray the tepid prayers we often pray. He prayed God-sized prayers. In one of the most spiritually nuclear passages in all the Bible he prays that his readers "may have strength to comprehend with all the saints what is the breadth and length and height and depth, and to know the love of Christ that surpasses knowledge, that you may be filled with all the fullness of God" (Eph. 3:18–19).

What exactly is Paul praying for? Not for greater obedience among the Ephesians, or that they would be more fruitful, or that false teaching would be stamped out, or that they would grow in doctrinal depth, or even for the spread of the gospel. All good things! But here Paul prays that the Ephesians would be given supernatural power—not power to perform miracles or walk on water or convert their neighbors, but power, such power, the kind that only God himself can give, strength to *know how much Jesus loves them*. Not just to have the love of Christ. To *know* the love of Christ. It's the difference between looking at a postcard of the Hawaii beach and sitting on that beach, blinking, squinting, absorbing the sun's warmth.

What is this love of Christ?

Niceness? Certainly not—this is the Christ who took the time to make a whip and then used it to drive the money changers from the temple, flipping over tables.

Is it a refusal to judge people? By no means: Scripture speaks of his judgment like a sharp two-edged sword coming out of his mouth (Rev. 1:16; 2:12).

The love of Christ is his settled, unflappable heart of affection for sinners and sufferers—and *only* sinners and sufferers. When Jesus loves, Jesus is Jesus. He is being true to his own innermost depths. He doesn't have to work himself up to love. He is a gorged river of love, pent up, ready to gush forth upon the most timid request for it. Love is who Jesus most deeply, most naturally is.

His Settled Heart, Our Settled Hearts

Your growth in Christ will go no further than your settledness, way down deep in your heart, that God loves you. That he has pulled you in to his own deepest heart. His affection for his own never wanes, never sours, never cools. That thing about you that makes you wince most only strengthens his delight in embracing you. At your point of deepest shame and regret, that's where Christ loves you the most. The old Puritan Thomas Goodwin wrote that "Christ is love covered over with flesh."[1] It's who he is.

Divine love is not calculating and cautious, like ours. The God of the Bible is unrestrained. If we are united to Jesus Christ, our sins do not cause his love to take a hit. Though our sins will make *us* more miserable, they cause his love to surge forward all the more. One day we will stand before him, quietly, unhurriedly, overwhelmed with relief and standing under the felt flood of divine affection in a way we never can here in this life. But in the meantime our lifeline to sustain us in this fallen world is that very love and our heart knowledge of it. Knowing this love is what draws us toward God in this life. We can revere his greatness, but it does not draw us to him; his goodness, his love, draws us in.

Blockages to Knowing His Love

And yet it often isn't that simple, is it? Some of us, no matter how much we try, no matter how much Bible we read, find the experience of God's love elusive.

Some of us look at the evidence of our lives, mindful of the pain we've endured, and we do not know how to respond except with cold cynicism. *The love of Christ?* we wonder. *Is this a joke?*

You're living in la-la land, Dane. This all sounds nice in theory. But look at the wreckage of my life. I know deep down in my bones I was created to be a palace, magnificent and stately. But I'm a pile of bombed-out rubble given the way others have treated me, wronged me, victimized me. My life disproves the love of Christ.

If you are having thoughts like that as you hear of Christ's love, I want you to know that you're looking at the wrong life. *Your* life doesn't *disprove* Christ's love; *his* life *proves* it.

In heaven, the eternal Son of God was "palatial" magnificence if anything ever was. But he became a man and, instead of ruling in glorious authority as one would expect of God-become-man, he was rejected and killed. His own life was reduced to bombed-out rubble. Why? So that he could sweep sinful you into his deepest heart and never let you go, having satisfied the Father's righteous wrath toward you in his atoning death.

Your suffering does not define you. His does. You have endured pain involuntarily. He has endured pain voluntarily, for you. Your pain is meant to push you to flee to him, where he endured what you deserve.

If Jesus himself was willing to journey down into the suffering of hell, you can bank everything on his love as you journey through your own suffering on your way up to heaven.

For others of you, it isn't so much what you have received at the hands of others but your own sin and folly that cause you to doubt God's love. You are a follower of Jesus and you keep messing up. You wonder when the reservoir of divine love is going to run dry.

Here's what I say to you: Do you realize how God treats his children who stiff-arm his love?

He loves them all the fiercer.

It's who he is. He is love. He is a fountain of affection. He is tireless, unquitting, in his embrace. Let him love you all over again. Pick yourself up off the ground, stop feeling sorry for yourself, and allow his heart to plunge you into his oceanic love more deeply than he ever has before.

Whether the wreckage of your life is your own doing or someone else's, you who are in Christ have never stepped outside the cascading waterfall of divine love. God would have to un-God himself for that deluge to run dry. You have muted your experience of his love. But you cannot stop the flow any more than a single pebble can slow Victoria Falls, a mile across and 360 feet high, as those millions of gallons of the Zambezi River come crashing over the cliffs there in southern Zambia.

Whether you have ignored it, neglected it, squandered it, misunderstood it, or hardened yourself to it—the Lord Jesus Christ approaches you today not with arms crossed but with arms open, the very position in which he hung on the cross, and he says to you:

None of that matters right now. Don't give it another thought.

All that matters now is you and me.

You know you are a mess. You are a sinner. Your entire existence has been built around you.

Step in out of that storm. Let your heart crack open to Joy.

I was punished so that you don't have to be. I was arrested so you could go free. I was indicted so you could be exonerated. I was executed so you could be acquitted.

And all of that is just the beginning of my love. That proved my love, but it's not an endpoint; it's only the doorway into my love.

Humble yourself enough to receive it.

Plunge your parched soul into the sea of my love. There you will find the rest and relief and embrace and friendship your heart longs for.

The wraparound category of your life is not your performance but God's love. The defining hallmark of your life is not your cleanness but his embrace. The deepest destiny of your life is to descend ever deeper, with quiet yet ever-increasing intensity, into the endless love of God. We grow spiritually by getting a head start on that project, right here in this fallen earthly life.

5

Acquittal

WE GROW IN CHRIST as we go deeper into, rather than moving on from, the verdict of acquittal that got us into Christ in the first place.

The gospel is not a hotel to pass through but a home to live in. Not jumper cables to get the Christian life started but an engine to keep the Christian life going.

Think of it this way: This is a book about sanctification. How do we move forward spiritually? And in this book on sanctification, this chapter is on justification. Sanctification is lifelong, gradual growth in grace. Justification, however, is not a process but an event, a moment in time, the verdict of legal acquittal once and for all. Why then are we thinking about justification in a book about sanctification? Here's why: *the process of sanctification is, in large part, fed by constant returning, ever more deeply, to the event of justification.*

But let's be more specific, bearing in mind that growth in Christ is a matter of transformation from the inside out, as opposed to merely externally oriented behavioral conformity. We could put the point of this chapter in three sentences:

1. Justification is outside-in, and we lose it if we make it inside-out.
2. Sanctification is inside-out, and we lose it if we make it outside-in.
3. And this inside-out sanctification is largely fed by daily appropriation of this outside-in justification.

Justification and Sanctification

First, justification is outside-in, and we lose it if we make it inside-out. In other words, justification is "outside-in" in the sense that we are justified by being given a right standing that comes to us from wholly outside us. This is strange and difficult to get our minds around at first. The very notion of a person's standing, an assessment of whether someone is guilty or innocent, universally depends on his or her own performance. Yet in the gospel we are given what the Reformers called an "alien righteousness" because the record of Jesus is given to us. In what

Luther called the "happy exchange," we are given Christ's righteous record and he takes on our sin-ridden record; accordingly, we are treated as innocent and Christ was treated as guilty, bearing our punishment on the cross. We are thus "justified"—that is, declared faultless with respect to our legal standing.

We resist this. Way down deep, we try to strengthen God's verdict over our lives through our own subtle contributions. But to do this is to turn justification from an outside-in truth to an inside-out truth. We lose entirely the comfort of justification if it is vulnerable to any self-strengthening. It must be all or nothing.

Sanctification, on the other hand, is inside-out, and we lose it if we make it outside-in.

Our growth in godliness, in other words, works in an inverse way to justification, both in how it works and in how it gets ruined. In our justification the verdict of legal acquittal must come wholly from heaven, landing on us as something earned by someone outside us, in no way helped out by our contribution. But that has to do with our *standing*. Sanctification, however, is change with regard to our *walk*, our personal holiness, the subjective result of the gospel. This must happen internally.

And just as we ruin the comfort of justification if we make it internal, we ruin the reality of sanctification if we make it external. But growth in godliness is not generated by conformity to any external code—whether the Ten Commandments or the commands of Jesus or self-imposed rules or your own conscience. This does not mean the commands of Scripture are worthless. On the contrary, they are "holy and righteous and good" (Rom. 7:12). But the commands of the Bible are the steering wheel, not the engine, to your growth. They are vitally instructive, but they do not themselves give you the power you need to obey the instruction.

Sanctification by Justification

And inside-out sanctification is largely fed by daily appropriation of outside-in justification.

The outside-in verdict nurtures the inside-out process. You can't crowbar your way into change. You can only be melted. Reflection on the wonder of the gospel—that we are justified simply by looking away from self to the finished work of Christ on our behalf—softens our hearts. The labor of sanctification becomes wonderfully calmed. The gospel is what changes us, and only it can, because the gospel itself is telling us what is true of us before we ever begin to change, and no matter how slowly our change comes.

We intuitively think that the way to grow is to hear exhortation. And exhortation has an important place. We are not mature Christians if we can never bear to hear the challenges and commands of Scripture. But the Bible teaches that healthy spiritual growth takes place only when such commands land on those who know they are accepted and safe irrespective of the degree to which they successfully keep those commands.

This need to return constantly to the freeness of the doctrine of justification must be emphasized because the fall rewires us to do precisely the opposite. Our fallen hearts are spring-loaded to assess our justified state on the basis of how our sanctification is going. But we grow in Christ by placing our sanctification in the light of our justification. The old English pastor Thomas Adam reflected on this truth in his diary, calling it "sanctification by justification." He wrote: "Justification by sanctification is man's way to heaven. . . . Sanctification by justification is God's."[1] In his classic work on union with Christ, James Stewart wrote: "It is God's justifying verdict itself which sanctifies. . . . It is precisely because God waits for no guarantees but pardons out-and-out . . . that forgiveness regenerates, and justification sanctifies."[2] Dutch theologian G. C. Berkouwer argues repeatedly throughout his study of sanctification that "the heart of sanctification is the life which feeds on . . . justification."[3]

Real Approval

Let's make this real practical.

Perhaps you believe in justification by faith but still find yourself lapsing back into, say, the need for approval from other people. Consider this: the most famous statement in all the Bible on justification by faith—Galatians 2:16—is brought to bear on the very same problem. Paul gives a teaching on justification not to unbelievers but to believers—indeed, to a fellow apostle, Peter himself. Why? Because Peter was "fearing" the circumcision party (Gal. 2:12). Peter had not settled in his heart what Paul had: "Am I now seeking the approval of man, or of God? Or am I trying to please man?" (Gal. 1:10). Paul identifies Peter's conduct as being out of step with the gospel (Gal. 2:14) and in violation of the doctrine of justification by faith (Gal. 2:16) because *Peter allowed the approval of people to erode his grasp of the approval that the gospel gives and the settled status that justification provides.*

At conversion we understand the gospel for the first time, and we feel the immense relief of being forgiven of our sins and granted a new status in the family of God. We learn for the first time that we are legally acquitted, innocent, free to leave the courtroom. But even for Christians, there remain regions within that continue to resist the grace of the gospel without our even realizing it. And one vital aspect of growing in Christ is coming back time and again to the doctrine of justification to do chemotherapy on the remaining malignancies of our craving for human approval.

Live your life out of the fullness of a justified existence. Let Jesus Christ clothe you, dignify you, justify you. Nothing else can.

Do you want to grow in Christ? Never graduate beyond the gospel. Move ever deeper into the gospel. The freeness of your outside-in justification is a critical ingredient to fostering your inside-out sanctification.

6

Honesty

TO THIS POINT we have been reflecting on what happens between God and me in fostering growth. But to these vertical realities we must join the horizontal. A Christian is connected not only *up*, to God, but also *out*, to other Christians. Scripture calls believers the body of Christ. We live our lives in Christ in a way that is vitally, organically joined to all other believers. We who are in Christ are no more detached from other believers than muscle tissue can be detached from ligaments in a healthy body.

The Bible has much to say about how we are to interact with each other as fellow Christians if we are to grow. I'd like to focus in this chapter on one particularly important teaching from the New Testament, the most important corporate reality for our growth in Christ: honesty.

Walking in the Light

The Bible says, "If we walk in the light, as he is in the light, we have fellowship with one another, and the blood of Jesus his Son cleanses us from all sin" (1 John 1:7). As the surrounding context makes clear, "walking in the light" in this text is not living in moral purity but rather *honesty with other Christians*. And what we must realize, if we are to grow in Christ, is that we are restricting our growth if we do not move through life doing the painful, humiliating, liberating work of cheerfully bringing our failures out from the darkness of secrecy into the light of acknowledgment before a Christian brother or sister. In the darkness, our sins fester and grow in strength. In the light, they wither and die. Walking in the light, in other words, is honesty with God and others.

We consign ourselves to plateaued growth in Christ if we yield to pride and fear and hide our sins. We grow as we own up to being real sinners, not theoretical sinners. All of us, as Christians, acknowledge generally that we are sinners. Rarer is the Christian who opens up to another about exactly *how* he or she is a sinner. But in this honesty, life blossoms.

Walking in the light is killing the preening and parading, the mask-wearing, the veneer, the keeping up of appearances. It is collapsing into transparency.

Everything in us resists this. Sometimes it feels like we would rather die. Actually, walking in the light is a certain kind of death. It feels as if our whole personhood, our self, is going into meltdown. We are losing our impressive appearance in front of another Christian. But what would you say to a baby terrified of being born, wanting to stay in the warmth and darkness of the womb, refusing to come out into the light? You would say: *If you stay in there, you will die. The way into life and growth is to come out into the light.*

Here's what happens when we begin to get honest, even with just one other person. The two circles of what we know ourselves to be and what we present ourselves to be overlap. Rather than the private Dane being one person and the public Dane a different person, there's just one Dane. We become whole. Integrated. Strong. But the keeping up of appearances is an exhausting way to live.

Honesty with each other has many powerful results. This verse mentions two:

1. We have fellowship with one another.
2. The blood of Jesus his Son cleanses us from all sin.

We'll take them in that order.

Fellowship with One Another

We were made to be together, to speak to each other, to share our hearts, to laugh together, to co-enjoy a beautiful flower.

The pain of a sorrow is doubled when endured alone but greatly lessened when borne by another alongside us; likewise the satisfaction of a joy is doubled when celebrated with another yet lessened when enjoyed alone. We pant for a bonded spirit with others, for shared hearts, for togetherness. Often our idolatrous pursuits through sexual immorality, overindulgence in alcohol, or social media platform-building are all simply misplaced longings for human fellowship. If we traced those heart-eroding pursuits down to their source, we would find, among other things, simply an absence of real Christian fellowship.

As we walk in the light with each other, the walls come crashing down. We relax into a new way of being, a liberated way of existing with one another. Fellowship ignites and burns brightly. We are actually able to enjoy others, instead of just using them or constantly being in impress mode. Indeed, keeping up appearances has become so normal to us, we don't even realize how deeply we're mired in it. Surely one of the shocks of the new earth, when all our fallenness and sin and self-concern has evaporated, will be the startling new freedom and pleasure of simply being around other people. Emptied of any need to present ourselves a certain way, we will have finally come truly alive. We will be free.

The message of the New Testament is that we can begin to enjoy that freedom—not perfectly, but truly—now. Which brings us to the second result of walking in the light.

Cleansing from All Sin

"The blood of Jesus his Son cleanses us from all sin." This little statement tucked into the back end of 1 John 1:7 is the whole reason any one of us will ever make it to heaven one day. We are cleansed by the blood of Christ. We are given a bath. A one-time, permanently effective, cascading cleansing.

We'll keep sinning in lots of ways, of course, but what is most deeply true of us is that we have been decisively washed clean once and for all. In culminating fulfillment of the shed blood of the Passover lamb in the Old Testament law, Jesus stood in for his people and let his own blood be taken on their behalf. He offered his own life so that all who desire for Jesus's blood to stand in for the taking of their own blood can have that substitutionary transaction determine their own eternal destiny. In that way his blood cleanses us. Jesus, the clean one, was treated as dirty so that I, the dirty one, am treated as clean.

Many of us feel irredeemably dirty. We know God loves us, and we believe we really are justified. But in the meantime we can't get out from under the oppressive sense of dirtiness. *The gospel answers that.* If you are in Christ, heaven has bathed you. You have been rinsed clean and are now "un-dirty-able." Jesus was defiled to free you from your defiled status and your defiled feelings.

A thoughtful reader may respond at this point: *The text says that "if we walk in the light . . . the blood of Jesus his Son cleanses us from all sin." Does that mean if we're not honest with each other, God won't cleanse us?*

We know from the broader teaching of the Bible that this is not so. The text means that as we walk in the light, the cleansing blood of Christ becomes more real to us. It moves from believed theory to felt reality. We experience that forgiveness more deeply than we otherwise can. Our hearts crack open to receive it more deeply than before. When you trust God enough to speak your sinfulness to another human, the channels of your heart are opened to feeling forgiven. This is because the same pride that stops us from confessing our sins to a brother or sister also hinders our felt belief in the gospel. Evading honesty before another Christian is more fundamentally a rejection of the gospel itself. Refusing to be honest with another is works righteousness in disguise; we are believing that we need to save face, retain uprightness of appearance. This is why confessing our sins to another naturally makes the gospel itself more real to us.

Collapse into Flourishing

Do you want joy? John did say, after all, that he was writing 1 John "so that our joy may be complete" (1:4). Do you want to grow? Perhaps just on the other side of real honesty with another Christian there awaits you a depth of "fellowship . . . with the Father and with his Son Jesus Christ" (1:3) that will make what you presently believe seem, in comparison, utterly unreal.

Believe the gospel. Find a trustworthy friend. Bring that brother or sister into your fallenness in a redemptive but humiliatingly transparent way. Humble yourself down into the death of honesty and see what life blossoms on the other side. Find yourself feeling bathed afresh in the gospel of grace. And as you dare to go deeper into honesty and deeper into the experience of the cleansing blood of Christ, watch your heart relax into the growth you long for.

7

Pain

MISERY AND DARKNESS AND ANGUISH and regret and shame and lament color all that we say, do, and think. The reality of nightmares shows that this pain and futility even reaches into our subconscious and our sleep. We can go *nowhere* to escape the futility and pain of life in this fallen world. Pain is not the islands of our life but the ocean; disappointment and let-down is the stage on which all of life unfolds, not an occasional blip on an otherwise comfortable and smooth life.

And a crucial building block in our growth in grace is a humble openness to receiving the bitternesses of life as God's gentle way of drawing us out of the misery of self and more deeply into spiritual maturity. Through pain God is inviting us up into "mature manhood, to the measure of the stature of the fullness of Christ" (Eph. 4:13; see also Rom. 8:17).

Slicing Off Branches

Each of us is like an otherwise healthy vine that has the perverse inclination to entangle all its tendrils around a poisonous tree that appears nourishing but actually deadens us. We have been told that touching this tree will kill us. But we can't help ourselves. We wrap ourselves around it. There's only one resort for the loving gardener. He must slice us free. Lop off whole branches, even.

The world and its fraudulent offerings are like that poisonous tree. The biblical category for this perverse inclination of our hearts to look to the things of this world to quench our soul thirst is *idolatry*. Idolatry is the folly of asking a gift to be a giver. The Bible tells us instead to locate our supreme longings and thirstings in God himself. He alone can satisfy (Ps. 16:11), and he promises he will satisfy (Jer. 31:25). And our heavenly Gardener loves us too much to let us continue to commit soul suicide by getting more and more deeply attached to the world. Through the pain of disappointment and frustration, God weans us from the love of this world.

When life hurts, we immediately find ourselves at an internal fork in the road. Either we take the road of cynicism, withdrawing from openheartedness with God and others, retreating into the felt safety of holding back our desires and longings, lest they get hurt again, or we press into greater depth with God than we have ever known. Either we smirk at what we said we believed about God's sovereignty and goodness, thinking that pain has just disproven what we said we believed, or we put even more weight on our theology. The two circles of professed theology and heart theology, to that point distinct, are forced either to move farther away than ever or to perfectly overlap. Either we let the divine physician continue the operation, or we insist on being wheeled out of the operating room. But pain does not let us go on as before.

If you want to be a solid, weighty, radiant old man or woman someday, let the pain in your life force you to believe your own theology. Let it propel you into deeper fellowship with Christ than ever before. Don't let your heart dry up. He is in your pain. He is refining you. All that you will lose is the Self and misery that in your deepest heart you want to shed anyway. God loves us too much to let us remain shallow.

Your tears are his tools.

Mortification

Alongside the kind of pain in which we are passive is another kind of pain in which we are active. I refer to the age-old discipline that theologians call mortification.

Mortification is just a theological word for "putting to death." It refers to the duty of every Christian to kill sin. As John Owen put it in the most important work ever written on killing sin, "Be killing sin or sin will be killing you."[1] None of us is ever in neutral. Right now, every one of us who is in Christ is either killing sin or being killed by sin. Either getting stronger or getting weaker. If you think you're coasting, you're actually going backward. It may feel as if you're currently in neutral, but our hearts are like gardens: if we aren't proactively rooting out the weeds, the weeds are growing.

Mortification is the most *active* facet of our growing in Christ. The verse on which John Owen based his book on mortification was Romans 8:13: "For if you live according to the flesh you will die, but if by the Spirit you put to death [i.e., mortify] the deeds of the body, you will live." As we find ourselves being pulled down by sin and temptation, we cry out to the Spirit for grace and help, and then we act in conscious dependence on that Spirit, taking it by faith that we are, thanks to the Spirit, able to kill that sin or resist that temptation. The devil wants us to think we are impotent. But if God the Spirit is within us, the very power that raised Jesus's dead body to triumphant life is able to exert that same vital power in our little lives (Rom. 8:11).

In speaking of pain as a vital ingredient to our growth, and especially now as we speak of our self-inflicted "pain" of mortification, we must be careful not to view the pain of our lives as in any way contributing to Christ's atoning work. That may sound obvious, but the temptation to do so is subtle and insidious. We must remember what we rehearsed in chapter 5 about acquittal. In the finished work of Christ on the cross we are completely liberated from the accusing powers of the devil and our own consciences. In killing sin we are not completing Christ's finished work; we are responding to it. Christ was killed so that our own relative success or failure in killing sin is no part of the formula of our adoption into God's family.

Suffocating Sin

How, practically, do we mortify sin?

We don't mainly kill sin by looking at it. We have to be aware of it, of course. But we don't kill sin the way a soldier kills an enemy in battle, by zeroing in on the enemy himself. Killing sin is a strange battle because it happens by *looking away from the sin*. By "looking away" I don't mean emptying our minds and trying to create a mental vacuum. I mean looking at Jesus Christ. In the same way that playing matchbox cars on the front lawn loses its attractiveness when we're invited to spend the afternoon at a NASCAR race, sin loses its appeal as we allow ourselves to be re-enchanted time and again with the unsurpassable beauty of Jesus.

We feed sin by coddling it, pining after it, daydreaming about it, giving vent to it. We suffocate sin by redirecting our gaze to Christ. As our hearts redirect their gaze to the Jesus of the Bible in all his glorious gentleness and dazzling love, sin gets starved and begins to wilt. As we enjoy the truths this book has been reflecting on—realities such as our union with Christ and his unshakable embrace of us and God's irreversible acquittal of us—then, right then, spiritual life and vigor begin to have the ascendancy, and the grip of sin loosens.

There is no special technique to mortifying sin. You simply open your Bible and unleash it, letting God surprise you each day with the wonder of his love, proven in Christ and experienced in the Spirit.

Fighting Is Winning

Are you struggling with sin today? The struggle itself reflects life. If we were not regenerate, we simply wouldn't care. The longing for Christ, the frustration at our falls, the desire to be fully yielded to God—these are the cries of life, even if immature life. God will not let you go. He will be sure to love you on into heaven.

In the meantime, he is teaching you not to give up your mortification project. Your very efforts to fight your sin distress

Satan. Fighting is winning. C. S. Lewis put it well in a January 1942 letter, and with this word of comfort we close this chapter:

> I know all about the despair of overcoming chronic temptations.
>
> It is not serious provided self-offended petulance, annoyance at breaking records, impatience etc doesn't get the upper hand. *No amount* of falls will really undo us if we keep on picking ourselves up each time. We shall of course be very muddy and tattered children by the time we reach home. But the bathrooms are all ready, the towels put out, and the clean clothes are airing in the cupboard.
>
> The only fatal thing is to lose one's temper and give it up. It is when we notice the dirt that God is most present to us: it is the very sign of His presence.[2]

8

Breathing

ALL THE CHAPTERS OF THIS BOOK till now have reflected on overarching themes. Realities such as union with Christ, or the embrace of Christ, or acquittal before God through the wonder of justification—these are timeless truths we spend a lifetime believing and absorbing into our hearts. But how, practically, day by day, do we do that? What are the actual tools by which that belief and heart absorption take place?

This chapter answers that question. In truth there are many valid answers to the question—the sacraments of the church, Christian fellowship, good books, and so on. But I want to consider just two ordinary, predictable, wondrous, vital practices: Bible reading and prayer.

And the way to think about these two practices is by the metaphor of breathing. Reading the Bible is inhaling. Praying is exhaling.

Our Greatest Earthly Treasure

What is the Bible? It is your greatest earthly treasure. You will stand in strength, and grow in Christ, and walk in joy, and bless this world no further than you know this book.

Scripture is not an ancillary benefit for a life otherwise well-ordered, in need of a little extra boost. Scripture is shaping and fueling.

How so?

Fallen human beings enter this world *wrong*. We do not look at ourselves correctly, we do not view God correctly, we do not understand the way to be truly happy, we are ignorant of where all human history is heading, and we do not have the wisdom that makes life work well. And so on. The Christian life—our growth in Christ—is nothing other than the lifelong deconstruction of what we naturally think and assume and the reconstruction of truth through the Bible. The Bible reeducates us. The Bible makes sages out of fools. It corrects us.

But the Bible not only corrects us; it also oxygenates us. We need a Bible not only because we are wrong in our minds but also because we are empty in our souls. This is why I like the metaphor of breathing. Taking a big breath into our lungs fills us with fresh air, gives us oxygen, calms us down, provides focus, and brings mental clarity. What inhaling does for us physically, Bible reading does for us spiritually.

In this shifty, uncertain world, God has given us actual words. Concrete, unmoving, fixed words. We can go to the rock of Scripture amid the shifting sands of this life. Your Bible is going to have the same words tomorrow that it does today. Friends can't provide that—they will move in and out of your life, loyal today but absent tomorrow. Parents and their counsel will die. Your pastor will not always be available to take your call. The counselor who has given you such sage instruction will one day retire, or maybe you'll move out of state. But you can roll out of bed tomorrow morning and, whatever stressors slide uncomfortably across your mental horizon as you groan with the anxieties of the day, your friend the Bible is unfailingly steady. Through it God himself draws near to you.

A Book of Good News

Many of us approach the Bible not as oxygenating, however, but as suffocating. We see the Bible lying there on the end table. We know we should open it. Sometimes we do. But it is usually with a sense of begrudged duty. Life is demanding enough, we think. Do I really need more demands?

That's an understandable feeling. But it is lamentably wrong. And it brings me to the central thing I want to say about the Bible as we continue to think about how real sinners get traction for real change in their lives. The Bible is good news, not a pep talk. *News.* It is reporting on something that has happened. The Bible is like the front page of the newspaper, not the advice column. To be sure, the Bible also has plenty of instruction. But the exhortations and commands of Scripture flow out of the Bible's central message, like ribs flowing out of a spine. Paul said that the Old Testament was written so that "through the encouragement of the Scriptures we might have hope" (Rom. 15:4). The Bible is help, not oppression. It is given to buoy us along in life, not drag us down. Our own dark thoughts of God are what cause us to shrink back from opening and yielding to it.

When we yawn over the Bible, that's like a severe asthmatic yawning over the free offer of a ventilator while gasping for air. Read the Bible asking not *mainly* whom to imitate and how to live but what it shows us about a God who loves to save and about sinners who need saving.

Every passage contributes to the single, overarching storyline of Scripture, which culminates in Jesus. Just as you wouldn't parachute into the middle of a novel, read a paragraph out of context, and expect to understand all that it means, you cannot expect to understand all that a passage of Scripture means without plotting it in the big arc of the Bible's narrative. And the main story of the Bible is that God sent his Son Jesus to do what Adam and Israel and we ourselves have failed to do—honor God and obey him fully. Every word in the Bible contributes to that message. Jesus himself said so (Luke 24:44; John 5:46).

Exhaling

And praying is exhaling. Breathe in; breathe out. We take in the life-giving words of God, and we breathe them back out to God in prayer.

How does prayer fit in to this book? This is a book on growing in Christ. And my resounding theme is that the Christian life is at heart a matter not of doing more or behaving better but of going deeper. And the primary emphasis I have wanted to give is that we grow specifically by going deeper into the gospel, into the love of Christ and our experienced union with him. As we now think about prayer, here is what we are doing: we are reflecting on the way our own souls must go out to God in Christ to desire, to long for, to receive, to dwell in, to thank him for his endless love. The gospel comes to us in the Scriptures, and in prayer we receive and enjoy it.

Put differently, to put prayer together with Scripture reading is simply to acknowledge that God is a real person with whom believers have an actual, moment-by-moment relationship. The Bible is God speaking to us; prayer is our speaking to him. If we do not pray, we do not believe God is an actual person. We may say we do. But we don't really. If we do not pray, we actually think he is an impersonal force of some kind, distant and removed. We don't view him as a *Father*.

What would you say to a ten-year-old daughter who never spoke to her dad, never asked him for anything, never thanked him, never expressed love to him, despite his many expressions of love to her? You could only conclude that she believed she had a father only in theory, not in actuality. You could only conclude that her father's love was not *real* to her.

Move through your day praying. Let God be your moment-by-moment Father (Rom. 8:15; Gal. 4:6). Hear his voice in Scripture in the morning, and turn that Scripture into prayer—and then let that time with him, that back-and-forth communion, send you off into your day communing with him all day long.

Inhale, Exhale

You wouldn't try to go through life holding your breath. So don't go through life without Bible reading and praying. Let your soul breathe. Oxygenate with the Bible; and breathe out the CO_2 of prayer as you speak back to God your wonder, your worry, and your waiting. Keep open the channel between your little life and heaven itself through the Bible and prayer.

As you do, you will grow. You won't feel it day to day. But you'll come to the end of your life a radiant man or woman. And you will have left in your wake the aroma of heaven. You will have blessed the world. Your life will have mattered.

9

Supernaturalized

THE FATHER ORDAINS SALVATION, the Son accomplishes salvation, and the Spirit applies salvation. In other words, there is no Christian life without the Spirit. The Christian life is purely theoretical if there is no operation of the Spirit. Everything that we *experience* of God is the working of the Spirit. That is true at conversion, as the Spirit opens our eyes to our sin and Christ's saving offer. And it is true of our growth.

The main thing I want to say in this chapter is this: because of the Spirit, *you can grow*. Those feelings of futility, the sense of impossibility, the settled resignation that you have permanently plateaued—that is not of heaven but of hell. Satan loves your shrugged acquiescence to your sin. Jesus Christ's heart for you is flourishing growth. He understands more deeply than you do the psychology of the heart fueling the sin you can't seem to leave behind once and for all. And he is fully equipped to walk you out of that darkness. For he has given you the most precious gift of all: his own Holy Spirit.

If you are a Christian, you are now permanently indwelt by the Spirit, and if you are permanently indwelt by the Spirit, then you have been *supernaturalized*. If you choose to stay in your sins, you won't be able to stand before God one day and tell him he didn't provide you with the resources.

Three Kinds of Men

But are there not plenty of decent human beings who are not indwelt by the Spirit, you may wonder? Certainly. That is because all people are created in the image of God, and by God's universal common grace he restrains much evil that would otherwise be executed.

But still, you might wonder, do we really need the Spirit in order to live a moral life? The answer is that we do not need the Spirit to live a moral life, but we do need the Spirit to live a supernatural life. In other words, we don't need the Spirit to be different on the outside; we do need the Spirit to be different on the inside.

So we can stiff-arm God by breaking all the rules, or we can stiff-arm God by keeping all his rules but doing so begrudgingly.

C. S. Lewis brilliantly captures this in his little essay "Three Kinds of Men." He says that there are not two but three kinds of people in the world. The first consists of those who live purely for themselves, and all that they do serves their own selfish cares. The second kind are those who acknowledge that there is some code outside them that they should follow—whether conscience or the Ten Commandments or what their parents taught them or whatever. Lewis says that people of this second kind see this other moral claim on them but feel a tension between that external moral claim and their own natural desires. As a result they are constantly swiveling back and forth between pursuing their own desires and following this higher claim. Lewis insightfully relates this tension to that of paying a tax—people in this second category pay their taxes faithfully but hope that something will be left over for them to spend on themselves.

Some people throw out all rules (group 1). Others try to keep all the rules (group 2). Neither approach is New Testament Christianity. The third kind of person is operating on a different plane entirely. Lewis puts it like this:

> The third class is of those who can say like St Paul that for them "to live is Christ." These people have got rid of the tiresome business of adjusting the rival claims of Self and God by the simple expedient of rejecting the claims of Self altogether.

The old egoistic will has been turned round, reconditioned, and made into a new thing. The will of Christ no longer limits theirs; it is theirs. All their time, in belonging to Him, belongs also to them, for they are His.[1]

Lewis goes on to conclude that it is simplistic to view only two kinds of people, the disobedient and the obedient. For we can be "obedient" in the sense that we follow a certain code, yet in a taxpaying kind of way. Authentic Christianity is not simply doing mechanically what God says but enjoying God. "The price of Christ is something, in a way, much easier than moral effort—it is to want Him."[2]

The point of this book on growing in Christ is to help Christians leave behind the second kind of person Lewis describes here and to be melted, more and more deeply, into the third kind of person. And here's the point: we only get from person 2 to person 3 through the Holy Spirit. To grow as a disciple of Christ is not adding Christ *to* your life but collapsing into Christ *as* your life. He's not a new top priority, competing with the other claims of reputation, finances, and sexual gratification. He is asking you to embrace the freefall of total abandon to his purpose in your life. And that is why the Holy Spirit dwells within you. He is the one who is empowering you to do what would be utterly impossible left to carnal resources—to step into the delicious, terrifying freedom of single-minded allegiance to Jesus.

It may feel impossible to you to do that. That's good. It *is* impossible. You'll never get there until you first try living for Christ out of your own strength and discover just how fearful and cautious and spiritually impotent you are on your own steam. It's then, as you give up on yourself and throw your hands up in the air, that your heart is most fertile for the supernaturalizing power of the Holy Spirit.

Closed vents can't be cleaned, full cups can't be filled, and the Spirit does not enter where we are quietly operating out of self-dependence. But the distraught, the empty, the pleading, the self-despairing, those tired of paying the tax of obedience to God and trying to live on what's left over—theirs are hearts irresistible to the humble Holy Spirit.

A Foretaste of Heaven

Keep in step with the person of the Holy Spirit. Ask the Father to fill you with the Spirit. Look to Christ, in the power of the Spirit. Open yourself up to the Spirit. Consecrate yourself to the beautiful Spirit's ways in your life. Recognize and believe way down deep in your heart that without the empowering Spirit all your ministry and efforts and evangelizing and attempts to kill sin will be in vain.

As you do so, you will be a little walking portrait of heaven itself to everyone around you. With lots of foibles and mistakes, for sure. And many lapses back into walking in the flesh—like Lewis's second kind of man. But here and there, at first for short bursts but gradually for longer stretches of your day, you will be learning to operate out of God's own divine resources. You will be giving people a taste of Jesus himself, the Lord whose Spirit has taken up residence within you.

Conclusion: What Now?

THE FINAL CONCLUSION, the deepest secret, to growing in Christ is this: look to him. Set your gaze upon him. Abide in him, hour by hour. Draw strength from his love. He is a person, not a concept. Become personally acquainted with him, ever more deeply as the years roll by.

It may seem, at this point in the book, that its nine chapters have given you a list of nine strategies to implement or nine different techniques to bear in mind. That's not at all what I want ringing in your heart as you close this short book. I do not have nine things to say. I have one thing to say. Look to Christ. You will grow in Christ as you direct your gaze to Christ. If you take your eyes off of Jesus Christ and direct your gaze to your own growth, you will prevent the very growth you desire.

On September 10, 1760, John Newton wrote to a "Miss Medhurst," who was one of a group of women Newton had visited in Yorkshire to offer spiritual counsel. Responding to her and her friends' request for help in going deeper with the Lord, he said:

> The best advice I can send, or the best wish I can form for you, is that you may have an abiding and experimental sense of those words of the apostle which are just now upon my mind—"*Looking unto Jesus.*" The duty, the privilege, the safety, the unspeakable happiness, of a believer, are all comprised in that one sentence. . . . Looking unto Jesus is the object that melts the soul into love and gratitude.[1]

My goal in this book has simply been to coach you into that single, simple, all-determining impulse of the heart: looking to Jesus. If you look to him, everything else is footnotes. All else will fall into place. If you do not look to Jesus, no amount of techniques or strategies will finally help you; all will be for nothing. Peel back every layer of distraction and look to Christ. Simplify your heart and all its cares. Look to Christ and his overflowing heart.

Let your union and communion with Jesus Christ, the friend of sinners, take you deeper, ever deeper, into the wonders of the gospel. And watch your heart, and therefore your whole life, blossom.

Acknowledgments

THANK YOU, MIKE REEVES, for inviting me to contribute this book to the Union series. This partnership, and the friendship it reflects, is precious to me.

Thank you, Davy Chu, Drew Hunter, and Wade Urig, brother pastors whom I revere, for reading and improving the manuscript. I love you.

Thank you, dearest Stacey, for insisting that I keep writing and for encouraging me all along the way. I adore you.

Thank you, Crossway, for your care of this project from start to finish.

Thank you, Thom Notaro, for your wonderful partnership in this project as its editor.

I dedicate this book to my seminary professors. When I landed on the campus of Covenant Theological Seminary in St. Louis in August 2002, I could hardly believe what I was seeing: men of God whose erudition and learning and commitment to the doctrines of grace *took them down deeper into humility and love*. I could have learned Greek anywhere; I could only learn interpersonal beauty fueled by Reformed theology at Covenant, under the faculty who were there at that time. They gave me a theological foundation for understanding how I grow as a Christian. But then, more wondrously, they gave me living pictures of what such growth blossoms into. In this Mordor of a world, I found myself in the Shire. What a mercy for God to send me there. I needed it. I still do. Thank you, dear fathers and brothers.

Notes

Chapter 2: Despair

1. *Letters of John Newton* (Edinburgh: Banner of Truth, 2007), 184.

Chapter 4: Embrace

1. Thomas Goodwin, *The Heart of Christ* (Edinburgh: Banner of Truth, 2011), 61.

Chapter 5: Acquittal

1. Thomas Adam, *Private Thoughts on Religion* (Glasgow: Collins, 1824), 199.
2. James S. Stewart, *A Man in Christ: The Vital Elements of St. Paul's Religion* (New York: Harper & Row, 1935), 258–60.
3. G. C. Berkouwer, *Faith and Sanctification*, trans. John Vriend, Studies in Dogmatics (Grand Rapids, MI: Eerdmans, 1952), 93.

Chapter 7: Pain

1. John Owen, *Overcoming Sin and Temptation*, ed. Kelly M. Kapic and Justin Taylor (Wheaton, IL: Crossway, 2006), 50.

2. C. S. Lewis, *The Collected Letters of C. S. Lewis*, vol. 3, *Narnia, Cambridge, and Joy, 1950–1963*, ed. Walter Hooper (San Francisco: HarperCollins, 2009), 507; emphasis original.

Chapter 9: Supernaturalized

1. C. S. Lewis, "Three Kinds of Men," in *Present Concerns* (London: Fount, 1986), 21. For similar articulations of what Lewis is after, though none quite as penetratingly clear as his, see Martin Luther, *Career of the Reformer III*, in *Luther's Works*, ed. Jaroslav Pelikan and Helmut T. Lehmann, 55 vols. (Philadelphia: Fortress, 1955–1986), 33:318; Luther, *The Christian in Society I*, in *Luther's Works*, 44:235–42 (cf. Luther, *Lectures on Galatians 1–4*, in *Luther's Works*, 26:125); Adolf Schlatter, *The Theology of the Apostles*, trans. Andreas J. Köstenberger (Grand Rapids, MI: Baker, 1997), 102; Geerhardus Vos, "Alleged Legalism in Paul," in *Redemptive History and Biblical Interpretation: The Shorter Writings of Geerhardus Vos*, ed. Richard B. Gaffin Jr. (Phillipsburg, NJ: Presbyterian and Reformed, 1980), 390–92; F. B. Meyer, *The Directory of the Devout Life: Meditations on the Sermon on the Mount* (New York: Revell, 1904), 148–51; Herman Ridderbos, *Paul: An Outline of His Theology* (Grand Rapids: Eerdmans, 1975), 137–40; Søren Kierkegaard, as quoted in Clare Carlisle, *Kierkegaard: A Guide for the Perplexed* (London: Continuum, 2007), 77–83; Martyn Lloyd-Jones, *Experiencing the New Birth: Studies in John 3* (Wheaton, IL: Crossway, 2015), 289.

2. Lewis, "Three Kinds of Men," 22.

Conclusion: What Now?

1. *Letters of John Newton* (Edinburgh: Banner of Truth, 2007), 47–48.

Scripture Index

Union

We fuel reformation in churches and lives.

Union Publishing invests in the next generation of leaders with theology that gives them a taste for a deeper knowledge of God. From books to our free online content, we are committed to producing excellent resources that will refresh, transform, and grow believers and their churches.

We want people everywhere to know, love, and enjoy God, glorifying him in everything they do. For this reason, we've collected hundreds of free articles, podcasts, book chapters, and video content for our free online collection. We also produce a fresh stream of written, audio, and video resources to help you to be more fully alive in the truth, goodness, and beauty of Jesus.

If you are hungry for reformational resources that will help you delight in God and grow in Christ, we'd love for you to visit us at unionpublishing.org.

unionpublishing.org

Union Series

FULL EDITION

Rejoice and Tremble

CONCISE EDITION

What Does It Mean to Fear the Lord?

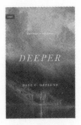

FULL EDITION

Deeper

CONCISE EDITION

How Does God Change Us?

The Union series invites readers to experience deeper enjoyment of God through four interconnected values: delighting in God, growing in Christ, serving the church, and blessing the world.

For more information, visit **crossway.org**.